My Grandmother's Veins

A J Roberts

BookLeaf
Publishing

India | USA | UK

My Grandmother's Veins © 2021 A J Roberts

All rights reserved.

No part of this publication may be reproduced, stored in a retrieval system, or transmitted, in any form or by any means, electronic, mechanical, photocopying, recording or otherwise, without the prior written permission of the presenters.

A J Roberts asserts the moral right to be identified as author of this work.

Presentation by *BookLeaf Publishing*

Web: www.bookleafpub.com

E-mail: info@bookleafpub.com

ISBN : 9789358362190

First edition 2021

Dedication

For Nancy. Thank you for everything.

Preface

This collection is an experiment for me as a writer. The challenge of 20 days to craft 20 poems was not enough to push me far enough outside of my comfort zone to feel in unknown territory, so I went further and challenged myself to write using methods that are alien to me and strictly keep editing to one thirty-minute session per poem. These poems are the results of this experiment. It will be exciting to see what sort of reaction these words receive from those exploring the pages, and I am very interested to see how I feel about these creations six months from now.

1

There ain't nothing like the First Time.
Second time spent with sloppy seconds
searching for the source of the
splendour that was the First Time.
Sixth time is a habit and I'm still chasing
the First Time.
Scientific changes with dose and dope
and finding the spark that was the First
Time.
Two dozen times and feeling rough.
Still chasing that First Time.
I know it happened, so why can't I find it
again?
Memory under lock and key.
Triple digits with nothing to show but
scarred-up arms, sunken eyes, and a
fervent passion for the First Time.

Years have passed with stories of back alleys, toilets, and abandoned buildings trying to find a way back to what I deserve as mine: the First Time.

2

Front row seats for all to see.
Click record and start the stream for the
great unwashed to get their thrills for
tips and bits at my expense. Spread
wide with a smile and let my actions
hide my feelings as another voyeur joins
the fray. Contort my body and push the
limits to hide my secrets from the fans
that beg for more before wiping the cum
from their hands and heading back to
their family life as if this performance
never happens. From behind the screen
I am told to keep going and go further
than last time. Smile wide and present
the side of me I was taught to hide as a
youth and deadhead the flowers that
have been taken from me.

3

Does your hair still catch the sun's rays?
Do your eyes still shine at the sight of
rain?

Our breathing patterns give me hope
our beating hearts are something I don't
want to be without

Perhaps our hearts still beat the same.

4

Rope swing from a tree;
you and I in springtide scents
behind your home.

The blue trampoline
that lived along the stone path
let us touch the clouds.

I long for your hand;
my favourite memories
of you and me. Us.

5

Through the clouds of gas and rivers of
tears
a solitary figure stood strong;
placing a flower in the barrel
                of a gun
                        in the wrong.
Their eyes were crimson; bloodshot,
and blood flowed from the shot prior.

A gaping hole would appear
in their lives, matching the
victim's chest.

Still,
a solitary figure stood strong;
even though the hot smoking barrel
was turned toward their head.

Would the solitary figure place

the flower in a barrel turned on

their foe, or let rage and vengeance take

hold and rue the day in the morning?

All eyes were crimson; bloodshot,

and tears flowed from the sights prior.

6

I trace my Grandmother's veins in the
back of my hands;
I'm not really sure what it means as I
definitely don't have her artistic talent.
Nor do I have her wisdom.
How are such veins smooth yet rugged
with experience?
Perhaps this is my inheritance.
Did my Grandmother see her
Grandmother's veins in herself?

Blood pulses in deep reds as arteries
reach out
Yet veins return to the source – blue –
gasping for air.
I see my Grandmother's veins and they
keep me steady
Ready to refuel with each breath.

Fragile paper skin lost and regrown, but the veins stay

A tattoo of nature.

Matriarchal guidance.

7

One.

Two. Three. Four.

Count the bricks once more.

Five. Six. Seven.

Eight.

I've carved the names of those I hate

on the grey clay dried to a crisp

in a feeble attempt to abate

the weight of the hate.

Nine. Ten.

A knock on the other wall teases me

for more as I know more exists

and more is certain and more

is all I crave within these walls.

Eleven.

Twelve.

Thirteen.

Pause. Close eyes.

Reflect on why I'm here.

I don't know why I'm here.

No one knows why they're here.

I lost count.

One.

Two.

Three.

Four.

8

Glacial waters

      Crisp and pure

            Touch

Babbling brooks

flood Baikal

       Dark waters rise

and fall

As moon

phases turn

With you I am warm.

9

As summer came and took its place

You went and forgot my face

It's been such a long winter

This winter has been so long

I saw you and them out on your lawn

You added darkness to my dawn

It's been such a long winter

This winter has been so long

I guess I went and screwed myself

again

I never seem to learn

I never realised that history repeats

Oh, God, I want to learn.

10

The heaving bosom of my Queen ripe

for the bite like the forbidden fruits from

a tree I hide within.

Venom seeps through the veins

circulating on every fluttered heartbeat

from the machine in her chest.

I hold her close, tight, feeling the rise

and fall of her sternum.

I hold tighter.

My Queen's breathing slows, and eyes

fall closed for one final time.

I retreat to the shadows and into the

night to savour the taste of this nectar

before the remorse slithers in and bitter

blood laces my tongue.

11

Will you still be the smoke that fills my
lungs?
Will your breath still be the mist that
always stings my lungs?
What will happen to the lust that lingers
on my tongue?
Will the space between your lips
remember how my tongue
would feel as passion filled our hearts?
Will I be a reminder of when we opened
our hearts
to each other and opened much more?
Who could possibly fill the space I left
on your bedroom floor?
I try, and I try, but I cannot replicate that
feeling.
Do you ever think back to living in that
feeling?

I will cherish the shiver you gift me
before sleep.
Will you still be the dreams that fill my
sleep?

12

I miss the 'you' I once knew;
I miss the way I knew me too.
I missed my youth and teenage years
and those are years I won't get back;

It's not poetic, it's devastating.

These tears in my eyes
make me partially blind
but I guess it's fine because
I'm not looking to find
anything other than self-acceptance
in my own mind,
and I've been told that comes with time.

The space in my head that
was once full of dreams is now
filled with fears and tears shed

over the lost years I should

have grasped with both hands.

Not much about time is kind.

Chances are, I will love you,

even when you change your mind

about me – about us – about 'we'.

It's not poetic, it's devastating.

13

Superfluous scars
Tattooed on fragile wrists
Look at yourself
What have you missed?

Superfluous scars
Marking essential veins
Forcing smiles
Hiding pain

Flowers still stand
After being damaged
They still stay
Beautiful

I need you like
I need water in my lungs
Fill me up

I'm breathless

I thought love
Was meant to be
Good.

14

It's 4 am and I feel like I'm zero degrees
stuck in bed with my chest pulled down
to my knees.
I hear you breathe as you're asleep next
to me
I wish I could sleep and find myself in a
dream.

Walk the streets in some kind of
midnight trance;
the moths on the streetlights perform
their thankless dance.
I hear you breathe as you're fast sleep
in your bed.
I wish I could sleep and find some
peace in my head.

I'm simply a fish – don't applaud me for
swimming.
You're perfection – always applauded
for winning.
Why must you feel the need to look
down on me?
A person who can tear me apart with
their lips.

I want you to want me; I want you to be
free.
I can't feel anything lately
except tightness in my chest
even when I try my fucking best.

You sit me down and ask, "do I want to
be normal?"
Honestly, no. Not for a minute. Normal
sounds awful.

I'll drift around these empty streets at
night

because even without you I'll be all right.

15

You are so warm

Like winter sunshine

You intoxicate me

Like the finest wine

I always stay in the same place

Because I'm too afraid of being alone

Being away from the warmth

Where I lay my head is my home

The mind replays

What the heart can't delete

Your face in my head

Keeps me from sleep.

16

I won't pretend
I know the feeling
I'll do anything
To stop you leaving

You've been through hell
Come out swinging
Cuts on your body
Soon stop stinging

Does it still hurt
When does it get better
Hold on to this
It's my final letter

You cut yourself
Which cut me too
I wish there was

More I could do

I don't know where we're going

I don't know what our lives might be

I don't know how our story ends

But you'll always have me as a friend

…How… how do I say…

Say that I… I miss you.

17

Sunday morning rains darken the ground and freshen the stagnant air that has surrounded me all week. Tiny streaks on the window of racing droplets distract me from the onslaught of screens that have surrounded me all week. Windows wide to let in the wind, rain, and the earth to break the barriers of walls and doors that have surrounded me all week. Barefoot outside as the fresh water clings to my skin washing away the stress and tension that has surrounded me all week.

Eyes closed.

Shoulders back.

I breathe.

I breathe again, deeper.

My lungs fill with hope instead of the

panic that has surrounded me all week.

18

Don't you see I gave you
more than my very best
I gave you all of me
and now I have nothing left

I'll bring you that piece of
paper with words you wrote
back from when you had
ruled the world

I'm not so cold
about anything anymore

Life is too short to
spend another day
at war with yourself
at war with myself

I am a work in progress

and that's okay

I want to give you more

I'll keep driving

until the exits

no longer remind me

of the small town where I'm from.

19

There is such convenience in regret
after the fact. At night in the moonlight,
all blood looks black. I stop by a house
that now stands hollow and gutted by
fire; it once birthed childhood memories
and a safe haven for you that morphed
into teenage years of tears and beers
and aspirations of what you would do
when you grow up. I follow the stone
path to the charred wood door and
stand motionless as I recollect how
good of a liar you were when you told
me you loved me and always would.

Do you keep me in mind from time to
time? Actually, what the hell am I doing,
this isn't about me. This is about your
life, not mine. How do you feel? Are you

doing fine, or have you managed to
surpass all expectations brought about
by your limitations as a kind and caring
individual? Just like our time together,
the nights are too hot, and the days are
too cold. I can't remember a word I've
been told about love. This is a good old
tragedy, not a romance or comedy.
Stand for the applause in the spotlight
as the curtain draws low and the
audience absently go towards the exit;
I'll join the crowd and file out in silence
to spot the moonlight making all blood
look black.

20

Coffee and cigarettes: breakfast of
champions
but I don't smoke and I only drink tea.

Flirting and innocence: the constant
game we play
but what are the rules and I'm guilty.

The world is big and I am not
but I am still enough.

The mind replays
what the heart can't delete:
Your face in my head
is keeping me from sleep.

I was your first; that meant I was the
best

but at the same time the worst.

21

Run. Run away. Keep running. Run to clear the mind. Run to find clarity. Run until you're breathless. Run to find some breathing space.

Run into the desert; forest; mountains; tundra – whatever you do: run.

Run from the noise and tantrum of the city. Run from problem people. Run when no answer can be found. Run to where no answers will be found. Run to the rhythm of your breathing and then keep running when your lungs burn and your ankles sprain. Run through the wall. Run. Run when blisters bleed and bones break.

Run. Run until you find the clarity.

I am sure you'll find the clarity.

I am confident you'll find the clarity.

Oh, God, I hope you find some clarity.